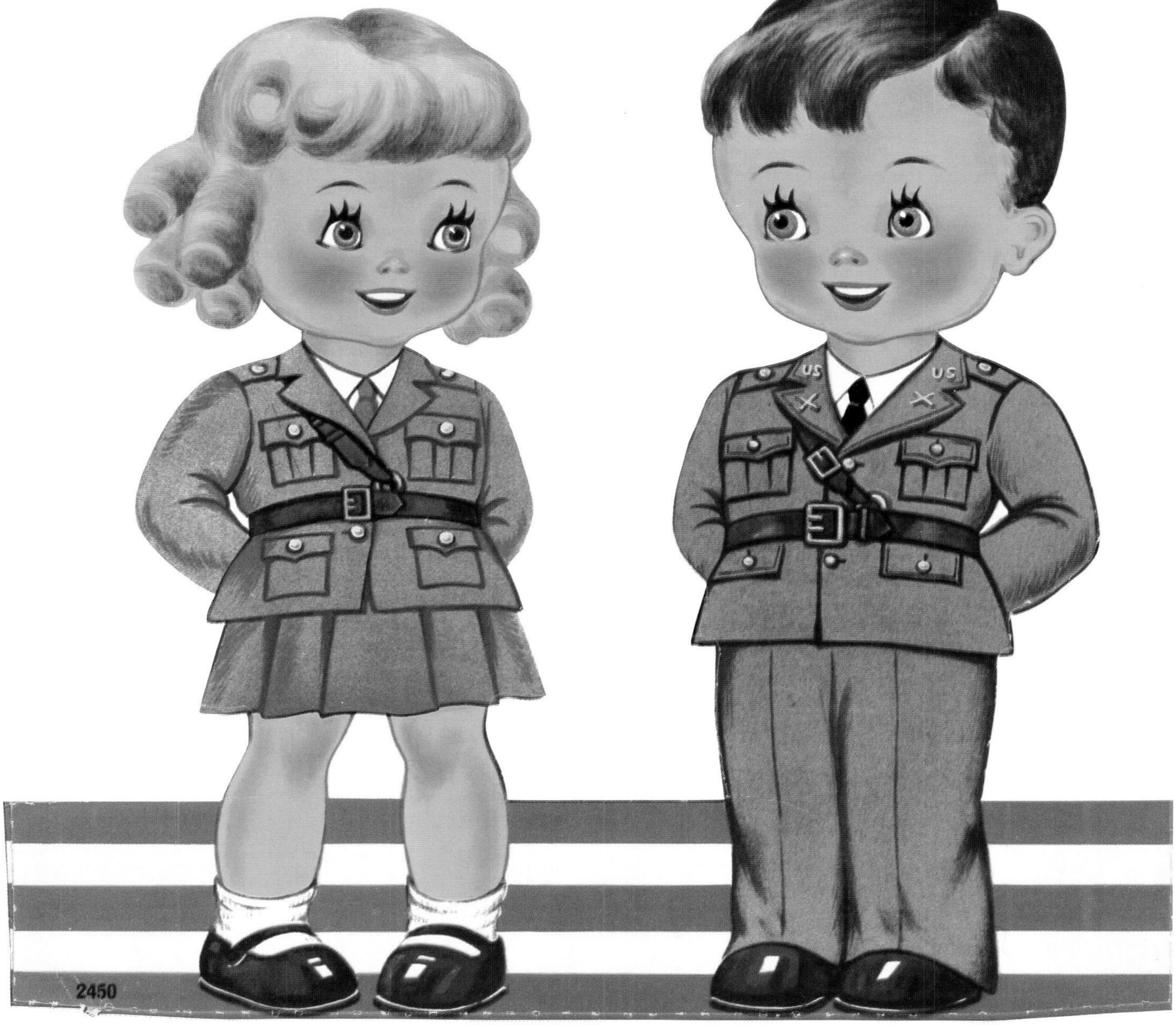
US
US
2450

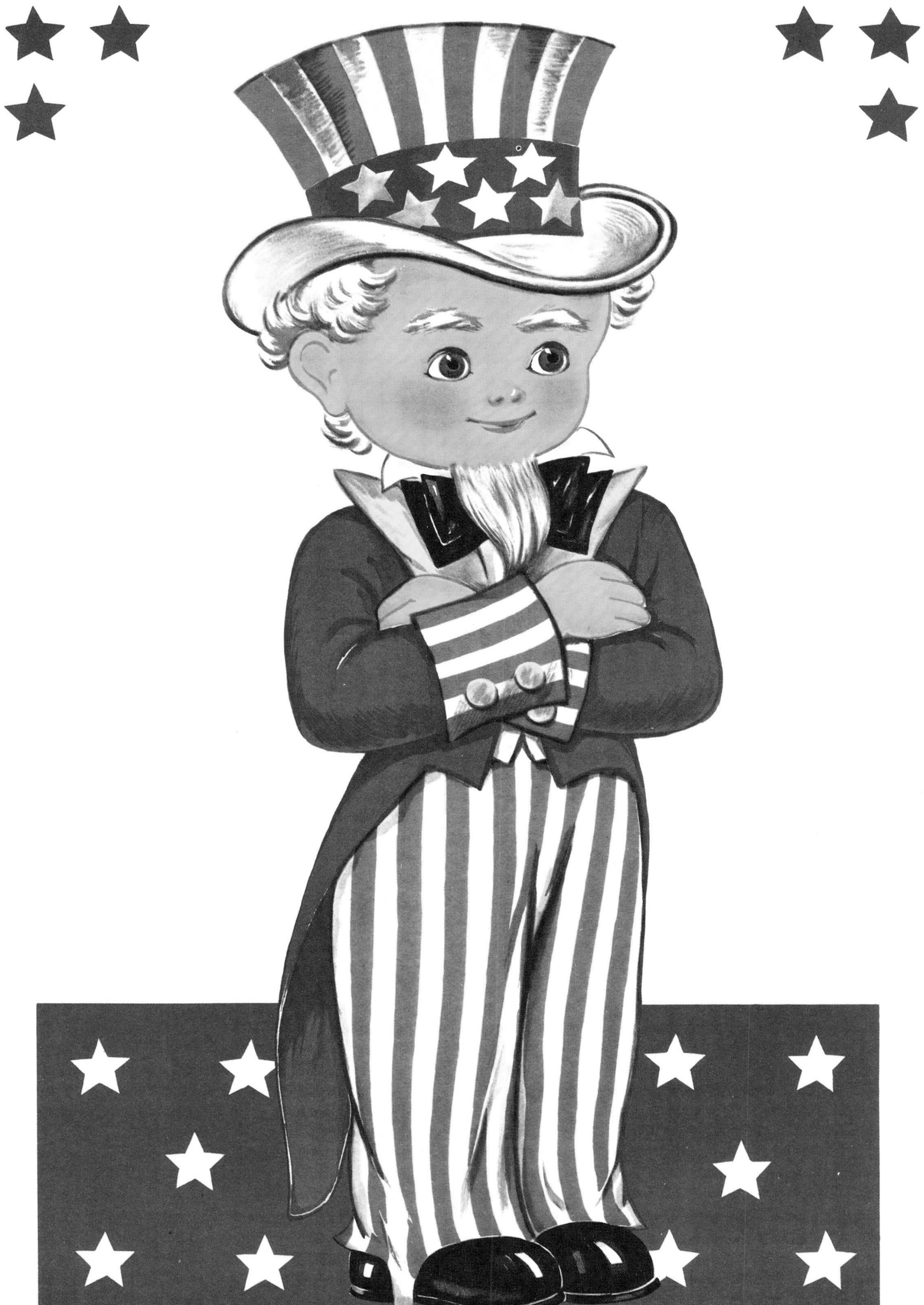

ENTERTAINMENT FOR SERVICE MEN

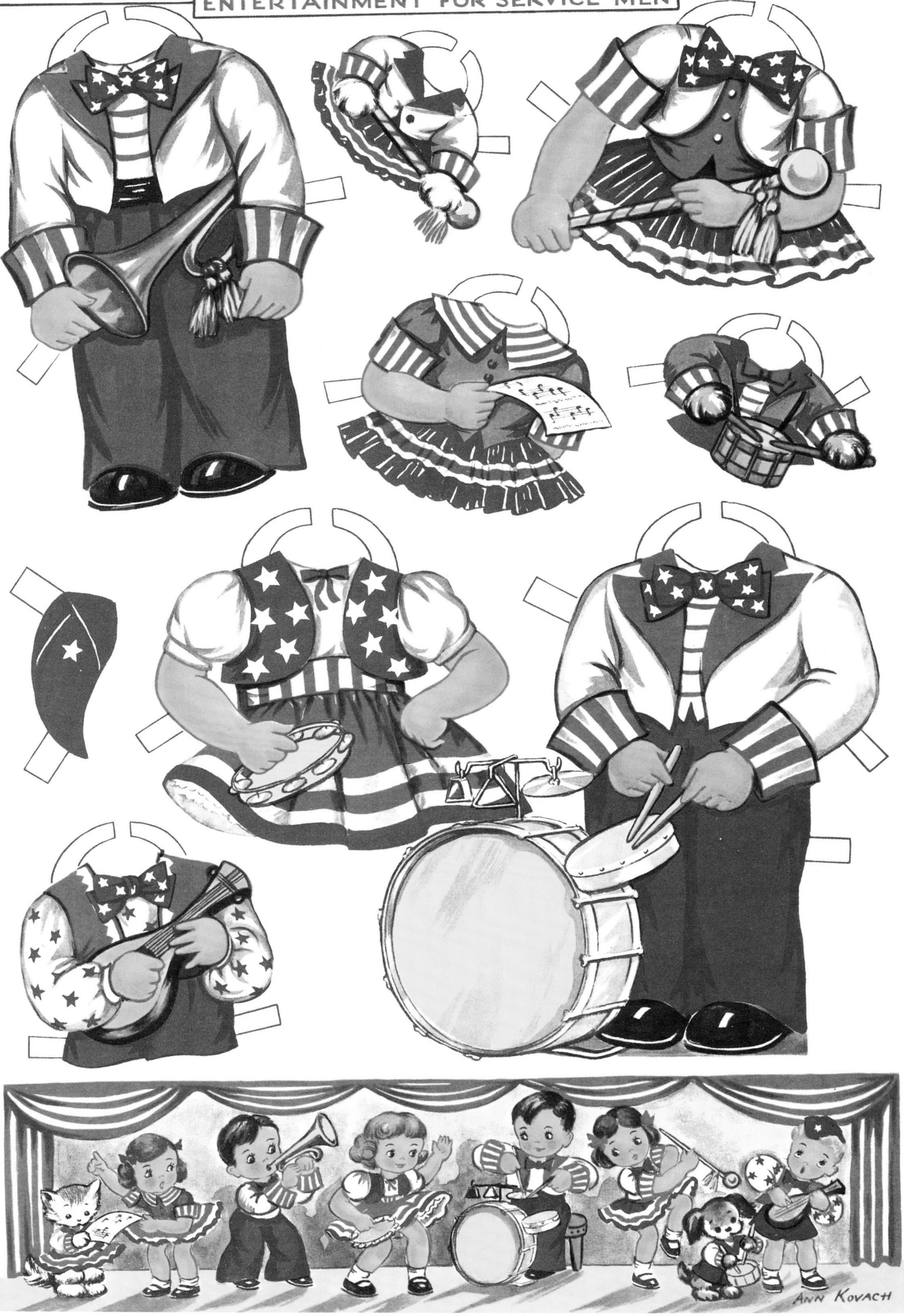

OUR VICTORY GARDEN

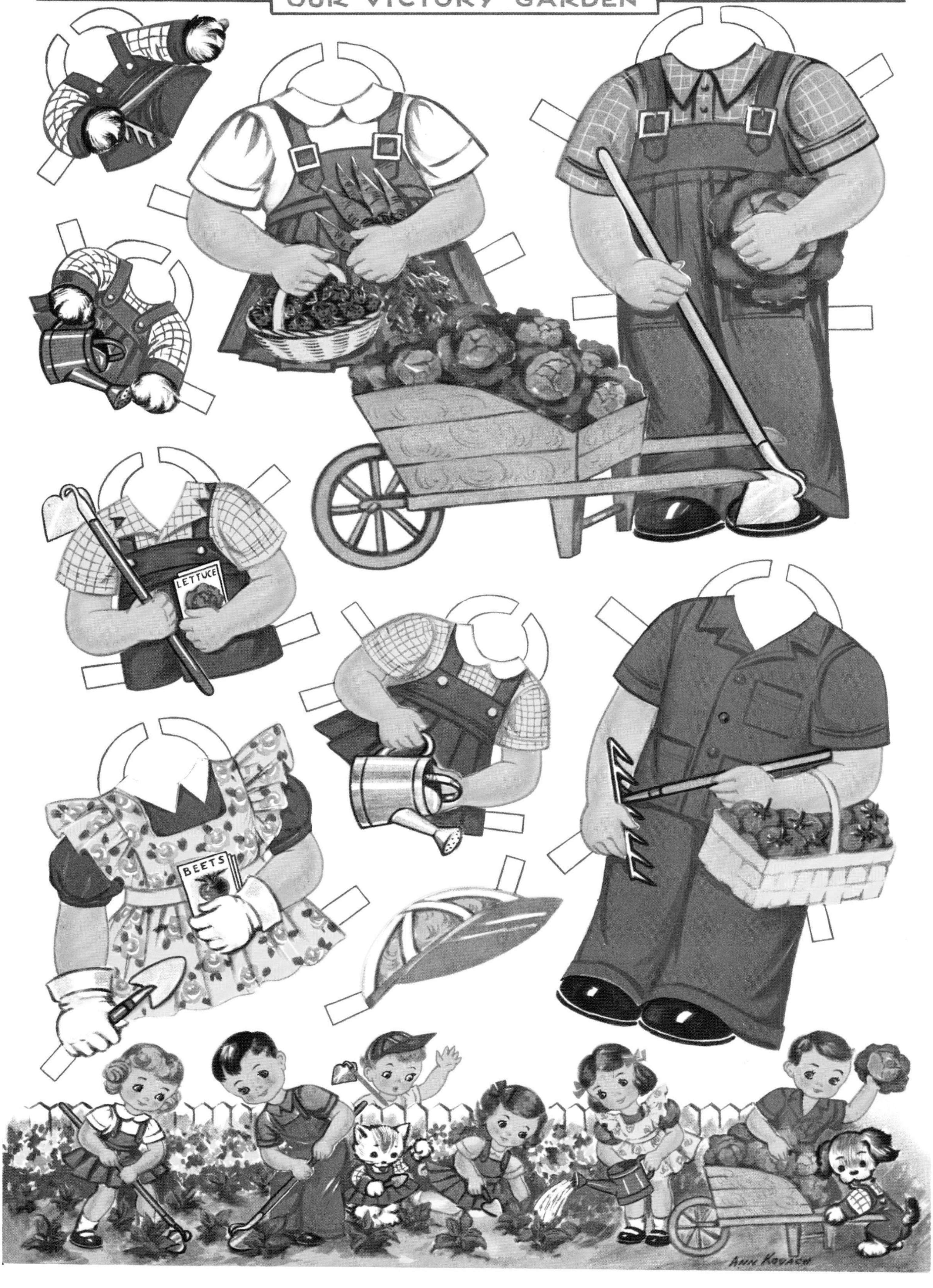

WE INSPECT

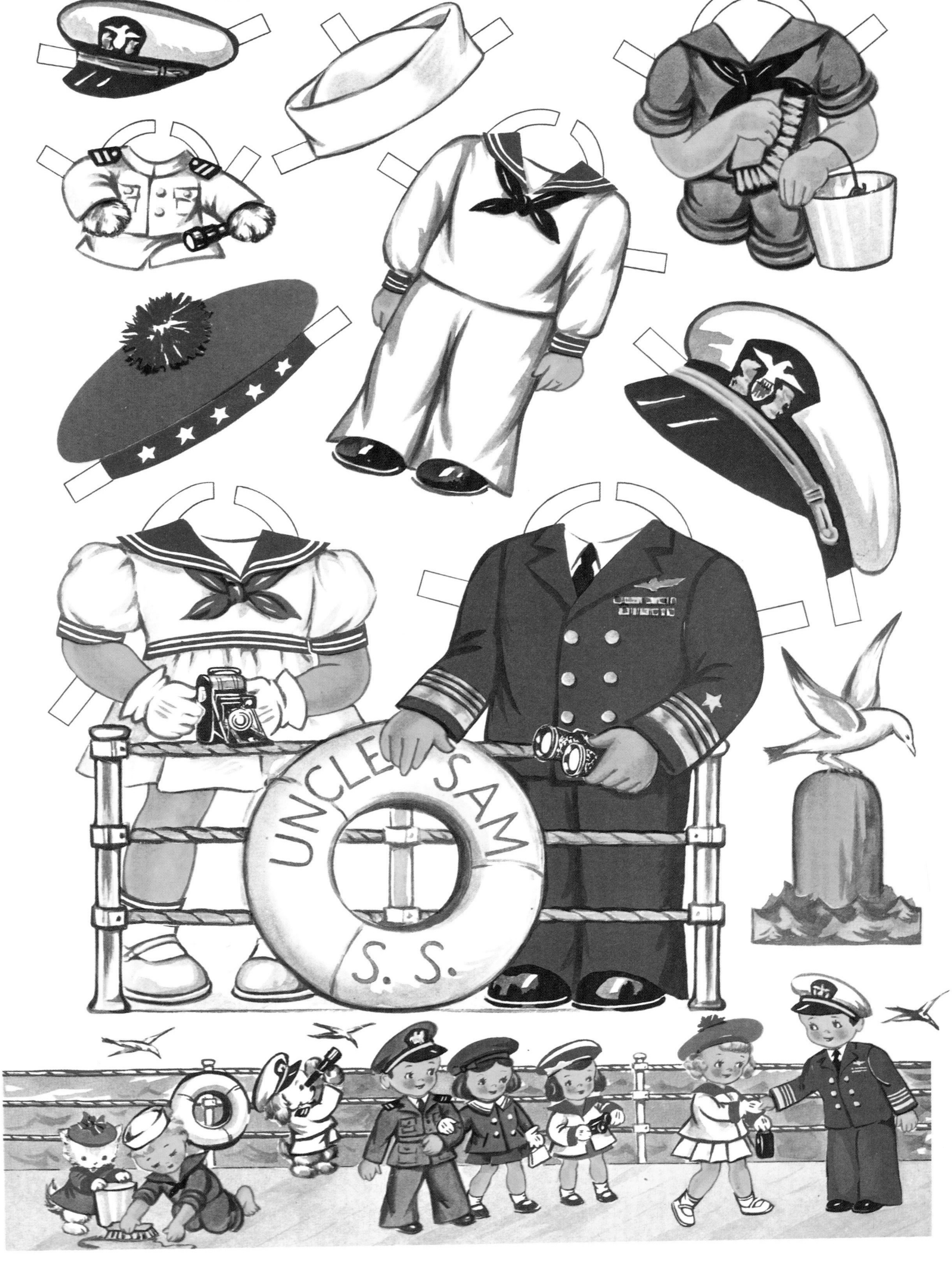

THE NAVY

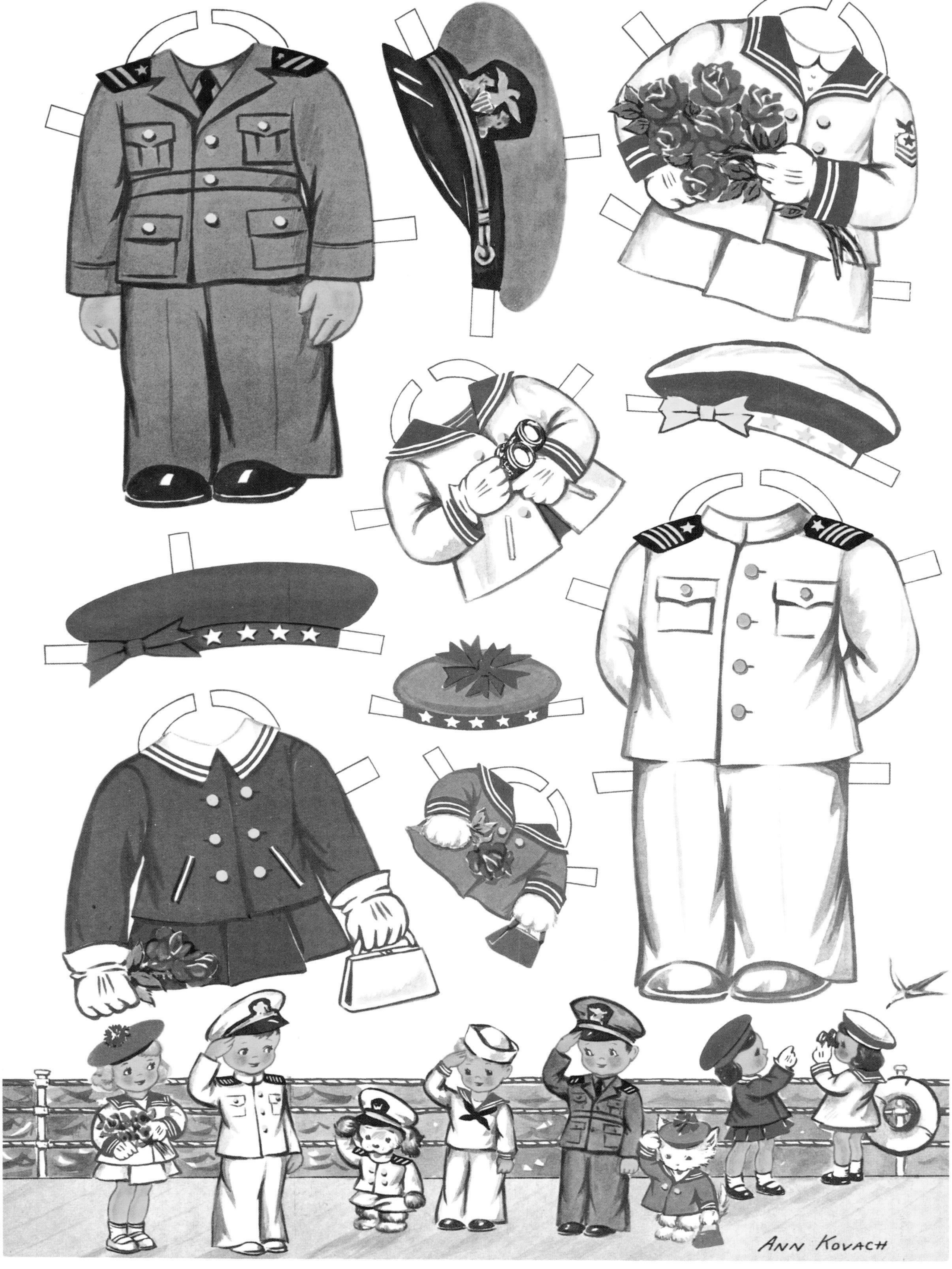

AT THE FLYING FIELD

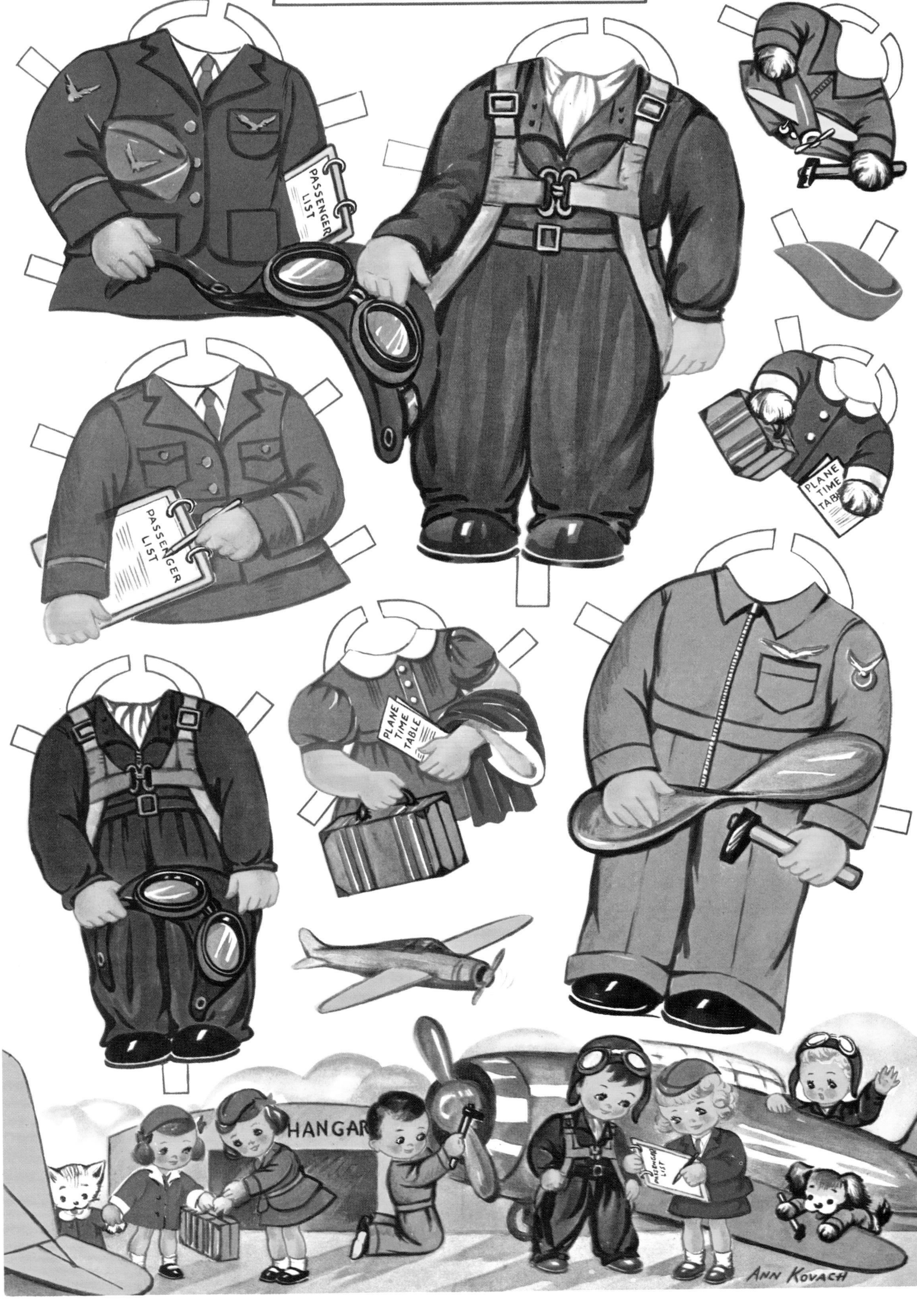

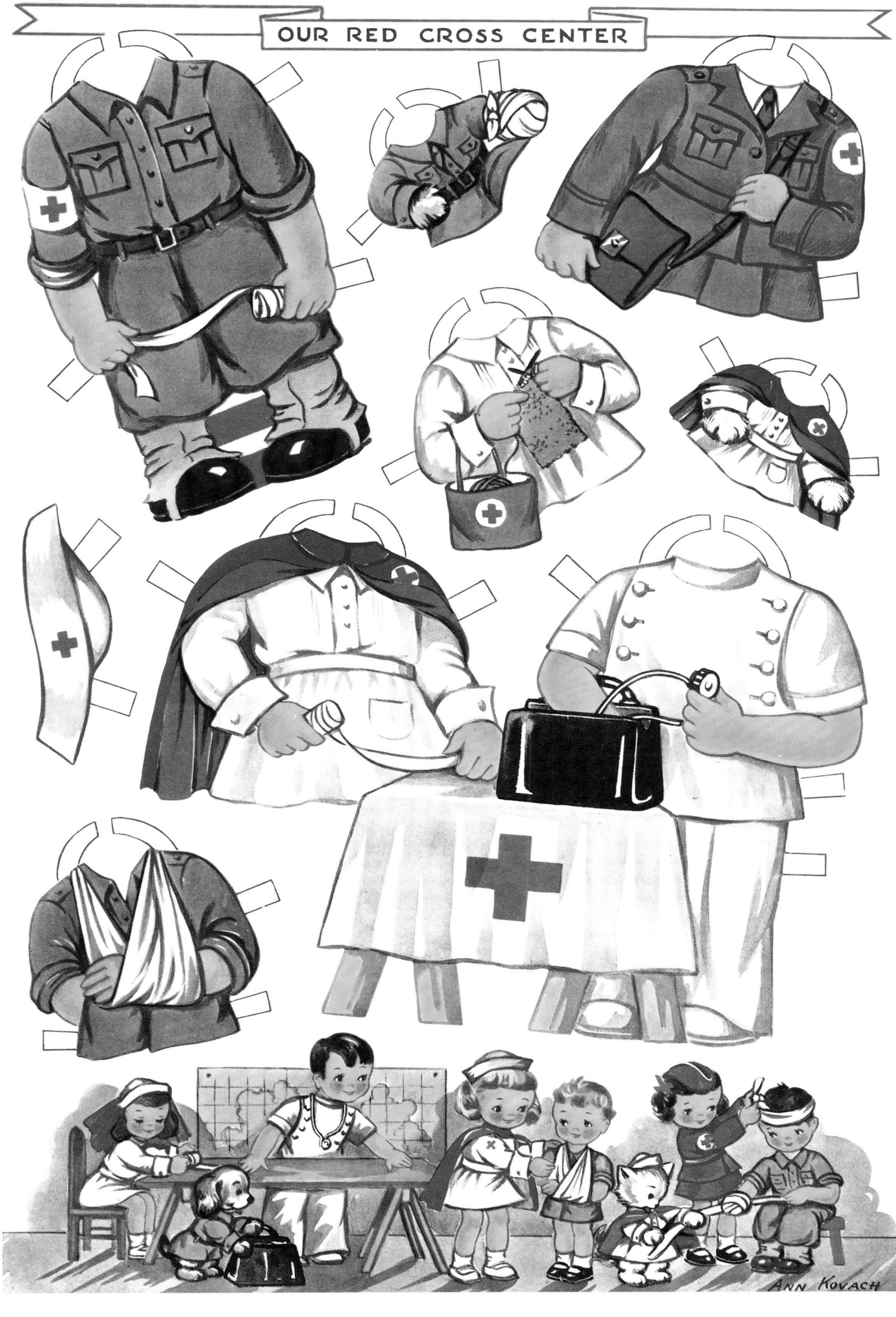
OUR RED CROSS CENTER
ANN KOVACH

OUR CANTEEN SERVICE

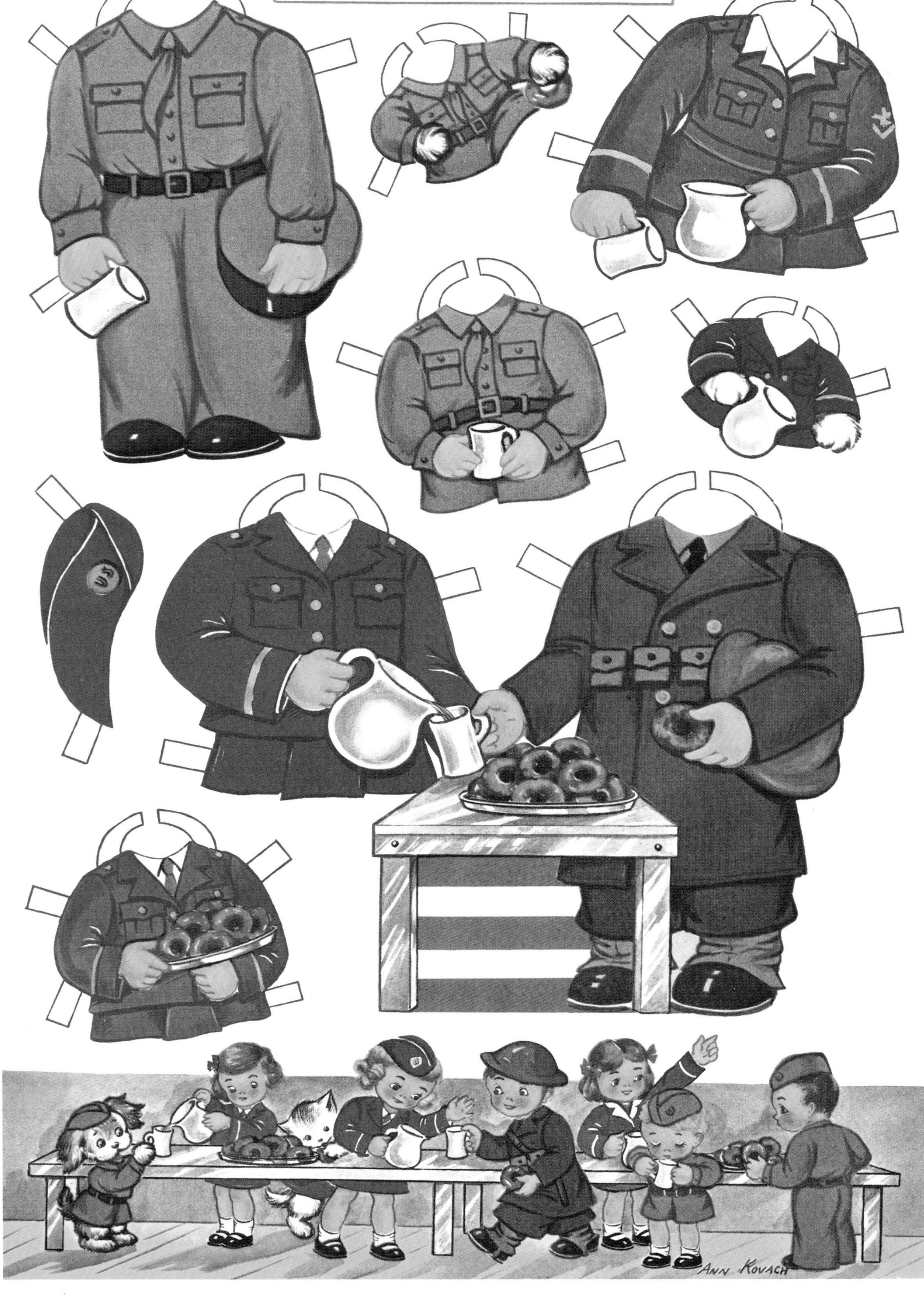